CONSUMER EMOTION LEARNING METHODS

JOHN LOK

ISBN 979-888569596-1

Contents

Foreword

keyword: Face Reading Technology, constructive consumers choice Process, Ethnographic research, technology acceptance model, emotional product, rational product, affective tests, materialism, functional MRI mind reading technology

Preface

This book concerns how to predict customer'
emotion to judge how to manufacture the right food taste
to let your consumers to like to eat your food as well as how to produce or design your products to sell to them successfully. I shall use three science and psychology ethnographic research and artificial intelligent facial machine methods to explain how to predict consumer individual behavior , which is more accurate and what their strengths and weaknesses differences.

I wrote this book for several reasons. I want to give my opinions to let businessmen to know how to predict consumer emotion to avoid the risk to spend excess to invent the new products or produce the bad taste foods or soft drinks to promote to enter to sell wrongly. This book teach you how to prepare to produce
your products or foods and choose which sale channels can raise your sale successfully. This book consists three sections: This three parts concern my three different psychological and technological methods to explain how to predict consumer emotion to achieve to reduce the risk to avoid to invent the new products or foods to sell unsuccessfully.

First part concerns how to use face reading technology predicts consumer emotion to predict how to do the
acceptable ingradients to produce foods to let
them to feel more enjoyable to eat sweet foods or drink soft
drinking as well as how to use video camera
to investigate to predict customer emotion
to find what factors had attracted them
to choose to buy the manufacturers' products to use and judge whether how to increase your product more attractive to win your competitors.

The second section concerns how to find both what
the worst attributed factor(s) had influenced the
consumers to be caused to decide not to choose
to buy your product as well as what the best attributed factor(s) had influenced the consumers to be caused to decide to buy your product in constructive choice process. I shall indicate how manufacturers can analyze to judge

whether what the best and worst attributed factor(s) are during every consumer chooses to buy which kind of product or food in constructive choice process.

The final third section concerns how to judge whether the online sale channel is more suitable or is not more suitable to compare to the visiting shop sale channel to let the product manufacturers to decide to choose to concentrate on selling their products from either of these two sale channels. Moreover, I shall indicate how to solve their website weaknesses to attract customers like to visit their websites to make final purchase decision more easily. Finally, I hope manufacturers can learn how to predict consumer emotion to decide how to invent your products to sell in the correct attitude to achieve to increase client numbers and you can learn whether you ought to choose to use which method(s) to predict your clients emotion before you invent your products or manufacture which taste foods to sell.

Prologue

Table of contents

Face reading technology and video camera camera consumer behavioral recording machine emotion method

● Recommendation of face reading technology is for confectionery food manufacturers at factory or office experiment and ethnographic consumer behavior video camera recording method is for product manufacturers at home

The impact of emotions on judges, evaluations and decisions have long been important to psychology and consumer behavior on consumption. I shall examine how distinct perspectives shape the processes of appraisal that lead to emotional experience and how different consumers might define happiness distinctly. I examine emotions that vary by positive, negative and mixed. I also suggest new ways to distinguish among emotions and to assess how new ways to consumers to aim to be discovered by better understanding how consumers manage their experience of emotion to achieve their own affective goals. In my report, I shall indicate three aspects to research. The first aspect, I indicate how one sample technology to detect consumer emotion to predict facial reaction, such as Noldus Face Reader technology is used orange juice, sweets and chocolates confectionery foods or drinks to detect young consumers' emotion whether who like or dislike to eat or drink different brands of confectionery products from whose facial reaction for factory or shop experiments.

Besides, how to use video cameras to record consumer individual behavior at home to predict why who choose to buy your product to help manufacturer, as you to predict why your clients choose to buy your products or choose not to buy products to use.

● Main Problem Being Addressed of face reading and video camera technology limits

Technologies that detect consumers' emotions can help companies to reduce the amount of money waste on unsuccessful product launches by stopping products before they are launched. Methods can be accurately measured consumers' feelings and emotion for a food or beverage product irrespective of consumer's ability to accurately articulate those feelings are needed in order to generate more accurate food and beverage product testing results. These methods will be based on the measurement of human physiology-most likely facial expressions, but they reveal intentionally hidden or subconscious emotions. In addition, the method may be able to decide emotions: Such as happiness, sadness, surprise, fear, anger feeling when one youth person eats a food or drinks beverage product. The first aspect main problem concerns how face reading technology can be measured to predict consumer acceptance level of confectionery foods or soft drinks from their face expression in the short time more absolutely. However, this face reading technology can't be used to predict any consumer's individual enjoyable acceptance satisfactory level when who uses any manufacturer's products in the short time.So face reading technology can not be used to predict any consumer's emotion to reflect to use any product more easily. Thus, I shall recommend how to use video camera recording ethnographic research method to find what factors to influence the consumer who decides to buy the product to use and evaluate whose satisfactory level to use the product at home. I concern how to use video camera to predict consumer individual behavioral process to find why who choose to buy the kind of product to evaluate the most absolute emotion response to find whether who satisfies or doesn't satisfy to use the product. Also how to use face reading technology to measure different level sugar elements to add the confectionery foods to detect the consumer's emotion whether who likes or does not like to eat the kind of confectionery food.

● Summary of ethnographic research
of facial reading technology and video camera technology

To detect consumer's emotion like or not like to eat the confectionery foods, e.g. soft orange juice, sweet and chocolates. The food manufacturer may attempt to use face reading technology to predict different level sugar elements to add its confectionery eating products to see consumer's different face impression to evaluate whether what sugar elements , e.g. how much weights are the suitable level to add to the kind of confectionery food. To detect buyer's emotion whether who enjoy or does not enjoy to use the manufacturer's product and to find what factor(s)can influence the consumer to choose to buy the product. The home product manufacturer may use digital cameras and computer recording method to record the volunteer daily routines filmed at home. It aims to detect consumer's individual using behavior to research whether what psychological factors are to influence who to choose to buy themanufacturer's product to use. Otherwise, Ethnographic research concerns how to use video camera to record consumers' behavior daily about one weeks. It aims to predict what factors case who to buy the kind of product. Hence, Confectionery manufacturers can use face reading technology to predict consumer emotion of satisfactory level to eat sweats, ice creams, chocolates, biscuits etc. sugar add confectionery. Home product manufacturers can use video camera technology to predict consumer emotion of satisfactory level to use products at home e.g. clothing, radios, televisions, furniture, sleeping beds etc. home daily useful products.

● Comparative Benefits / Advantages

Face reading technology can help only confectionery eating food manufacturers to measure sugar element whether how much sugar weights are the most suitable to young people taste acceptable level more absolutely. Digital camera and computer recording technology can predict whether what factors can influence the consumer to choose to buy your competitor's similar product or your products and measure whose satisfactory level to let manufacturer to judge how to manufacture whose products of features are more suitable to be acceptable or attractive to consumers' taste.

If the confectionery eating food manufacturer could not detect consumers' emotion to know whether what level of sugar ingradient is the most suitable level to cause who are like or dislike to eat or drink confectionery foods from whose face expression absolutely. It will be serious loss to invest time and money to manufacture this foods and consumers will feel their foods or soft drinks is not health to eat to cause illness possibly. Traditional sensory and consumption tests predict consumer acceptance of new food products rather poorly, as are evidenced by the high their failure rates in the market. These tests typical reflect conscious processes whereas consumer acceptance may also be based on unconscious processes. For example, I feel functional (MFR) isn't an allowable technology space primarily due to consumer concern of manipulation. Miller (2012) indicated that " functional MRI mind reading technology is where something is wholly subjective and private, and it can't be predict consumer emotion to tell from what who're doing or looking at, what whose mental state is." Hence, It has a distinction between that kind of mind reading and what is brain reading, which essentially involves using brain scans to figure out what the factors can influence on consumer's mind in different situations to decide buy or not buy the food product. So, any consumer emotion researcher needs to wait a few seconds to see what consumers will do next. The technology is still limited, such as individual differences: Different consumers' brains code information sight differently, so consumer emotion researcher needs to learn how a specific individual codes consumers' emotion mental states. How to produce the most acceptable sugar level to manufacture any confectionery eating food or drink for children, it can keep consumers who will choose to buy other brands of confectionery eating food or drink more easily. This is the most important factor to influence your children taste choice to feel your brand confectionery eating food or drink is the best taste to compare other brand competitors. So, sugar ingradient (element) of the acceptable level is the most important research from face reading technology experiment in shop or factory.

The Netherlands (2014) indicated "Arnade had been carring to investigate consumers (man age 22 years) were recruited at the kaunas University of Technology. They were asked to rate the sample and then are characterized by Face reader program (Naldus Information Technology) Wageningen. The measurements are showed significant differences between facial expressions by the different samples of tested sugar element confectionery products and reflected liking ratings well. The positive correlations of facial expression happy and negative correlations of sad expression are predicted. It suggested that these may be the most valuable descriptors for explaining the quality of sweets and chocolates. It can be concluded that Noldus face reader technology is sufficiently accurate for differentiating between sugar confectionery products and can deliver additional information to conventional acceptance tests. " Otherwise, reasons for likes or dislikes of different foods or drinks are typically difficult to articulate, but may determine much of our food or drinks choice. Certain foods or drinks can be more active than other foods or drinks because for some reason who make consumers feel good when their express positive emotion. Arnade (2014) examined "consumers' facial reaction by the flavor of orange juice drinks using face reader technology measurement showed significant differences between facial expressions by the different samples. The explicit measurement reflected the liking ratings well. Especially expressions happy with liking and were good indicators for liked and liked samples respectively, 20 minimize artefacts, caused by the face reader software as emotion, they used liquid samples (juice) which need less processing in the mouth than solid samples." The aim of this work was to examine whether facial expressions measured with the Noldus face reader technology are a sufficiently accurate measure for differentiating between various types of sugar element confectionery including sweets, chocolates and juice drinks or soft drinks which need sugar element to add in the manufacturing processing and to investigate whether facial reactions are able to explain such these confectionery foods or drinks liking ratings. The impact of emotions on judge , evaluations and decisions has long been important to psychology and consumer behavior on consumption. It seems face reading technology can predict whether the consumer likes or dislikes these confectionery foods, chocolates, sweets or juice, soft drinks liking ratings to measure whether sugar element is excess or less from young consumers' face expression, such as enjoying or not enjoying of feeling, smile or no smile response. Hence, face measuring technology can be more difficult to detect consumers 'emotion for product manufacturer. Because consumers need to spend more time to attempt to use their new innovative products.

● Recommendation Ethnographic consumer behavior research is for video camera recording to product manufacturers at home

Otherwise, it seems product manufacturers can't use face reading technology to detect consumers' emotion in the short time immediately. The products include any kind of products, e.g. high technological products, such as space mining of resources machines, satellite navigation system ,cars , machines etc. as well as home useful technological electronic products, such as mobile phones, washing machines, televisions, laptops as well as daily products, such as shirts, shoes, furniture, toys, tooth pastes etc. These essential home product and high technologic product manufacturers who need to continue to innovate their old style products to follow consumers' taste to invent new style products to be accepted to their fresh taste. It seems that manufacturers need to spend a long time to touch consumers' feeling whether whose old style technological products which are still accepted to them to use or not. Hence, it implies that a consumer decides to buy these high technological innovation products, whose choice isn't performed to show who must accept to use these high technological innovation productsfor long time, whose emotion is not sure whether who feels satisfactory to consume to use this product for a long time. When he/she uses this technological product for a long time, it is possible that who will feel it was not valuable to buy it before. Hence, video camera can used to record the consumer's behavior record whose image and to analyze whose facial expressions and bodily gestures at home about one week.

● How to use video camera recording to predict consumer's emotion .

How to use automated facial expression analysis for emotion and behavior prediction. The expression of emotion is achieved through combinations of verbal and nonverbal information produced from various sources of the body and the brains. Nonverbal information encompasses any message that is not expressed in words, including gestures, postures to be performed from individual behavior for individual daily life. Though people often don't invest much thought to the nonverbal aspect of communication to be performed to manage emotional experiences. Computers enable researchers to process to gather data in a short amount of time to predict facial expression consumers. The new methodological for social scientists may be a valid analysis to automated facial expression from consumer's daily behavior at home experiement for several days investigation more absolutely. Among the various models of nonverbal communication, we focus on facial expression which are captured by small digital cameras and later analyzed with computer software. As Webb et. al. (2000) pointed out, "people are low-fidelity observational instruments recording and interpretation may be erratic over time, as the observer learns and responds to the research phenomena he or she observes. It means that we can observe consumer behavior to predict why who buy the product from whose daily life behavior performance. Recent studies applied automated feature extraction and classification to extract macro features . Such as the head and hand position and angle from video features taken during an experiment where a theft took place. It also implied that computer models obtained up to 71 percent correct classification of innocent or guilty participants based on the macro features extracted from the video camera. Furthermore, in an overview of detection research." Meservy et al.(2008) noted that "the accuracy of humans coding behavioral indicators only falls around 50 percent, but that computers trained to a automatically extract and identify relevant behavioral cues detect deception with significantly higher accuracy. Furthermore, computers operate without the other methods(e.g. physiological measures such as polygraph machines or lie detectors) and the lost of extensively trained human interviewers." Ambady and Rosenthal (1992) showed that "another advantage of why automated facial detection technology coupled with computational models is that once the system secures the parameters for a model, prediction of behavior (vs simple detection and classification) can be made using only a small sample. This is a computational recording of what social psychologists, a way people sample a short except from social behavior to draw inferences of about states, traits and other personally relevant characteristics .For instance, based on an observation of a three minute video clip of a conflict between a married couple." Carrere and Gottman(1999) also indicated "video cameras were able to predict the outcome of that marriage after six years. Using machine learning coupled with computer vision allows computers to cause this human cognitive process; models are trained on a short sample of facial features and those features automatically predict future behaviors. Computers were used in place of human coders to detect vocal behaviors (e.g. time spent speaking, influence over conversation partners, variation in pitch and volume and behavior mirroring) during a negotiation task. Their results imply that the speech features extracted during the first five minutes of negotiation are highly predictive of future outcomes." The researchers also noted that using computers to code speech features offers advantages such as high test-retest reliability and real time feedback. As a cost-effective and relatively accurate method to detect, track and create models for behavior classification and prediction, automatic facial expression analysis has the potential to be applied to multiple disciplines. Capturing behavioral data from participants may be a more accurate representation of how and what they feel, and a better alternative to self-report questionnaires that interrupt participants' affective cognitive processes and are subject to bias .Our model goes beyond to predict the future behavior within a given task (e.g. a virtual car accident or an error in performance). This opens up the possibility of such models becoming a common methodology in social scientific and behavioral research.

Installing video camera recording at sample consumers to carry on investigating their feeling to use their product to collect the more truly acceptable or not acceptable feeling to use the product reason, such as: video camera recording method is data synchronization and time series statistics calculation. In the next phase of analysis, video recording are recording with data collected from experimental tasks such as surveys or simple motor tasks. This is done to map the extracted facial geometry information to behavioral output data. In the experiments three to five second intervals of facial expressions were taken one to two seconds before each instance of the behavior to be predicted and used as the input data. After data synchronization we also computed a series of time-domain statistics on coordinates in each interval to use as additional inputs to our classifiers. For example one sample investigating. The input data for this study consisted of videotapes of forty one participants watching films that elicited the emotions of either amusement or sadness, along with measures of their cardiovascular activity responding. It should be noted that the recorded expressions were expressions, unlike the photographs of deliberately posed faces often used in prior facial expression research. However, I suggest these entertainment product or home product manufacturers who can use video cameras to record whose buyers' behavior to detect whose emotion to aim to design which kind of colors, styles, sizes and how to change whose old products' features to attract the more consumers' fresh demand taste .

Ethnographic research is interpretative research which seeks an understanding from the perspectives of the value systems of those being researched. Ethnographic search is one different method to learn about buyer individual behavior to compare with enquiring questionnaires to participants to fill to answer questions to gather data to carry on the sale and post purchase evaluation cycle to evaluate whether what are their product criteria or weaknesses which need to improve to raise their sale competition in their market. Palmer (2012) reported " one sport shoe company's ethnographic research in action was provided by a product commissioned by the footwear brand Dr Martens. It aims to research how to understand young people's buying behavior. It wanted to understand how youth people used brands in their every lives. Why for example, did some brands , such as Nike trainers or baseball caps become popular in youth culture? The researchers identified groups of young people around the world who responded to Dr Marten's target market. In return for a payment, volunteers were followed for several days and their daily routines filmed with a handheld digital camera. In total, 180 hours of captured film was edited to just one hour of highlights showing the key drivers of youth culture which are relevant to the Dr Martens brand. It seems that young people preferred fashions that allowed them to customize an item of clothing and in some way take ownership of it. The research drew the conclusion that iconic fashion items for young people had to have a distinctive label or style that made their wearers stand out as part of a tribe." Hence, ethnographic research seems to help this company to know why the young clients choose to buy those brands sport shoes, it is possible that the these brands sport shoes' color or design can be accepted more to them to buy Dr Marten brand's sport shoes when they wear different style of clothing. Hence, it uses digital cameras to observe the worldwide choice of paying target youth volunteers whose daily individual behaviors at homes to get the more actual evidence to evaluate what factors influence youth clients choose to buy these brands of sport shoes. It seems this sport shoe company can take several hours of filming to yield just a few moments of true insights to participant's true attitudes and behavior. Ethnography is one of many approaches that can be found within Social research. Ethnography was a descriptive account of a commonly or culture. Ethnography usually involves the researcher participating in people's daily lives for an extended period of time, watching what happens, listening to what is said, and/or asking questions through informal and formal interviews collecting documents. In more detailed terms, ethnographic work usually has most of the following features: People actions are studied in every contexts rather than under conditions created by the researcher, in experimental or high structured interview situations as well as data are gathered for a range of sources including documentary evidence of various kinds, but participant observation and/or relatively informal conversations are main ones as well as data collected is for the most past relatively unstructured in two senses and it doesn't involve following through detailed research design at the start and the categories that are used for interpreting what people say or are not built into the data collection process through the use of observation schedules or questionnaires to analyze. Generally, fairly small scale perhaps a style setting or group of people. This is a facilitate in depth study and analysis of data involves interpretation of the meaning, functions and consequences of human actions and low are implicated in local and perhaps also wider contexts what are produced for the most part are verbal descriptions, explaining and theories and statistical analysis play a subordinate role at most. How ethnography can learn more about buyer behavior to help product manufacturers to detect consumers' emotion. It means collection of data to pursue an answers to these questions more effectively and to test those against evidence. Hence, video camera recording to consumer's individual useful behavior at whose home. It isn't set up for research purposes (such as experiments or formal interviews). The methodological model for social research is physical science conceived in terms of the logic of the experiment. However, ethnography was sometimes dismissed as quite inappropriate to social science on the grounds that data and findings it produces are subjective. Hence, ethnographic research is the role to learn more about buyer behavior through marketers may have been listening more to consumers (e.g. through qualitative research), efforts have almost always been directed at controlling consumers ranges of products or services predetermined by producers have been pushed through with littler real involvement of consumers in the process at a time in which consumers are ever more aware of what is being done to marketers. To seeing consumer's daily life behavior can predict why who choose to buy your or your competitor's product. Then, the product manufacturer can judge what the reasons are caused to attract the consumer chooses to buy the product to use. Hence, the data analysis procedure will include these steps as below:

● First step, Facial expression videos camera record activity ; input data from given tasks will be carrying on researching at the same time.
● Second step, the feature extraction will be caused
● Third step, the chi-square feature selection will be caused
● Fourth step, the machine learning training will be caused
● The final step, the results of behavioral prediction and data classification will be output at the same time.

   ● Why ethnographic research can be predicted consumer's behavioral performance to detect emotion by video recording camera at home ? Ethnographic field research involved the study of groups and people as go about every day lives. There has two distinct activities. First the ethnographer enter into a social setting and gets to know the people and observes all the approach. But second the ethnographer writes down regular systematic ways what who observes and learns when participating in the quality rounds of life of others. Thus, the researcher creates an accumulating written records of these observations and experiences. Two interconnected activities comprise the care of ethnographic search: participation in some initially familiar social world and the production of written accounts of that world by drawing upon such participation. Hence, ethnographers are committed to get close to the activities and everyday people. Getting close minimally requires physical and social proximity to the daily rounds of people lives and activities, the field researcher must be able to take up positions in order observe and understand whom.

Consumer behavior refers to the behavior that consumers display in searching for purchasing , using , evaluating and disposing of products and services that who expect will satisfy their needs and it's behaviors that are directly involved in the action of obtaining, consuming and spending products or services, including the decision processes that precede and follow these actions. It seems ethnographic research can helps the marketer to understand how consumer think, feel and select from alternative like products, brands and the like and how the consumers' buying behaviors are influenced by their environment, the reference group, family and salespersons. Consumer buying behavior includes that: Attitude itself is a learning experience and can lead to a change in attitude before buyers enter the buying process. Thus, attitude don't automatically guarantee all types of behavior. Attitudes based on behavioral learning follow beliefs, behaviors and effect sequence. A consumer who is high involved with a product or service category and who perceives a high level of product or service differentiation between alternatives with follow the cognitive hierarchy (belief affect behavior). From the ethnographic research marketers perspective the sequence of attitude formation is from a communication point of views from a strategic point of view, such as it has proved useful in specifying the different elements that work to influence buyers' evaluations of attitude, product or services may be composed of attributes or qualities, some of which may be more important than others to particular people. So consumer's individual decision is to act on whose attitudes is affected by other factors, such as whether it is felt other factors, such as whether it is felt that buying a product or service would be met with approval by friends and family. According to this approach, ethnographic research marketers must concentrate an assessing the characteristics of the environment, such as the physical surroundings and product or service placement, that influence members of that target market. Such as point of purchase (such as selling the sport shoe brand's some sample of design style shoes) are particularly useful in predicting to find reasons why individual consumer choose to buy these styles. Hence, I recommend ethnographic research marketers can focus on measuring consumers' effective emotion response to products or services and develop offering that elicit appropriate subjective reactions and employ effective symbolism to predict how the different brand products to be designed which kind of style, to be used what kinds of colors and what kinds of materials to be produced. To decide which is the most acceptance to satisfy consumers' taste. Such as the above sport shoe brand company case showed that it attempted to use ethnographic method to research whether what the external or internal factors are influenced to the footwear brand Dr martens' other consumers to choose the Nike or Baseball brands sport shoes to buy. It discovered that what youth people whose daily wearing clothing colors, designs and materials external factors which can influence them to choose to buy which kinds of design styles, colors and materials made of sport shoes to buy. It seems famous brands of sport shoes and cheaper price and durability internal factors are not the important factors to influence them to choose to buy these brands. Otherwise, the youth people whose wearing clothing colors, design styles and material made external factors can influence their feeling to choose the most adaptable style of sport shoes to be accepted to adapt to accept to their wearing clothing fashion. Thus, it seems that ethnographic research is one good method to detect consumers emotion whether the individual consumer's choice is influenced by the product's internal factors more or external environment external factors more to influence every individual consumer to feel positive or negative emotion to make final decision to buy any product to use possibly. If the product manufacturer can use this ethnographic research method to attempt to find whether what external or internal factors can influence potential consumers' fashion acceptance level to choose to buy any new innovative products to predict their emotion before the new peoduct manufacturer decides to manufacture its products to sell in this competitive market. I believe that its predicting market success chance will be increased.

CHAPTER TWO

Online consumption machine predictive method

● Explaining what situation makes the individual consumer doesn't accept to use internet technology sale channel to buy the product as well as it why internet will cause negative purchase emotion to any consumer to choose to buy any manufacturer's products .

The third aspect solution, I shall explain why the electronic commerce sale channel in technology acceptance model, it is possible that why it can influence the consumer's positive emotion to be changed to be negative emotion to choose not to buy the manufacturer's product . Moreover, I shall teach manufacturer whether how to judge it ought or does not ought choose this technology model to sell its products from internet channel.

● Main Problem Being Addressed

The third aspect main problem is researched why internet sale will have what bad factors to influence consumers to cause negative emotion to decide not to buy manufacturers' products from online shopping. I shall recommend how to predict their products whether which are suitable to sell from internet and how to improve their sale methods to increase consumer's positive emotion to accept to buy their products from internet. The final discussion is judged in what situation it will cause individual consumer doesn't like to enter the manufacturer's website to choose to buy the manufacturer's products. I shall also indicate why the manufacturer will cause negative emotion to whose consumers if who chose online sale channel. I aim to teach manufacturer how to know whether whose products ought or not ought to be chose to sell from online sale channel as well as how to reduce to cause bad influence to consumers' emotion from whose websites to avoid online sale failure chance. I shall use internet surveys to gather information to detect whether what factors influence the consumer choose prefer to buy or not to prefer buy the manufacturer's products from internet as well as how manufacturers can predict consumer's emotion in the constructive consumer choice process before who choose online shopping. Hence, if the manufacturer could predict whether what weaknesses are existed to reduce whose website attraction to whose consumers' attention. It will avoid whose online sale failure. The benefits to manufacturer include who can predict what weaknesses of whose website are, then who can attempt to revise which aspects of whose website weaknesses in order to raise whose consumers' positive emotion when who uses internet to enter the sale website to find any kinds of products to buy them. If the manufacturer's website can raise attraction ability to increase many customers to see whose website. Then, whose customer numbers will be increased possibly. Online sale influence research can only apply to manufacturers who sell their products from their website sale channel.

● Related Background of internet sale channel

Nowadays, many young people like to choose to use internet to buy any manufacturer's products. Although internet is popular to accept to young to use to buy any products, but it will have chance to cause negative emotion to individual consumers from positive emotion due to they enter any manufacturer's website to find some bad points to influence their feeling to be bad. Finally, the consumers will not choose to buy the manufacturer's products due to the manufacturer does not know what the bad points are existed to whose website. Thus, I believe that internet won't be accepted to be the best sale channel to adopt to use to sell to any manufacturers' products effectively, even internet sale channel will cause some consumers negative emotion to influence who choose not to buy the manufacturer's products if the product's manufacturer chooses internet to help who to advertise whose this product to sell from internet sale channel.

Previous research has linked the experience of loneliness with materialism, suggesting that when consumers attach too great an importance to possessions, they may reduce the importance of their social relationships, leading to isolation and feelings of loneliness. Thus materialism may arises a way to cope with loneliness, which suggests that to decrease materialism, one may want to first focus on building social relationships and reducing loneliness rather than focusing first upon reduced consumption. Hung & Mukhopadhyay (2012) examined the influence of actor versus observes perspectives on the emotional experience. "They find that "actors tend to focus move on the situation at hand and experience more emotion, such as excitement, sadness when who recall or anticipate emotional experiences. Their previous research has linked experiences of loneliness with materialism, suggesting that when consumers attach to great an importance of their social relationship, leading to isolation and feelings loneliness. This may unfortunately, lead to downward, thus it focus on building social relationship and reducing loneliness rather than focusing first upon reduced consumption." It seems social environment can influence the consumer's social emotion to choose to consume the product. The meaning of happiness that is most relevant to influence choices, such select those with a present focus will prefer products that offer calm. Thus, it seems excited consumers will choose exciting products and calm consumers will choose relaxing products. It implies that who will prefer to choose to buy the kind of product from online shopping if the consumer is a excited person to accept new technology shopping model and enjoyed to loneliness to sit down to use whose laptop to choose to buy any online products at home quiet environment. Otherwise, if consumers don't like loneliness, who will like to leave their homes to go to retail shops to buy any manufacturers' new innovate products with their friends or families and who will feel more happy and enjoyable in this non technological shopping model. Thus, it implies the enjoyable quiet environment, loneliness, technology excited consumers will choose to buy products from online sale model more. Otherwise, the enjoyable noise environment, social relationship, calm consumers will choose to buy products from traditional retail shops sale channel. Thus, consumers' emotion will be influenced to feel enjoyable or non-enjoyable to buy the product from the online shopping model or traditional visiting retail shops model .It seems that noise or quiet shopping environment will influence individual consumer's emotion to make final decision to buy the product. If the consumer enjoys to choose to buy any brands of products in the quiet environment at home lonely, the online shopping technological model will be more chance to be accepted to make final decision to this consumer habitually. Otherwise, if the consumer enjoys to choose to buy any brands of products in the noise environment, social relationship with friends, the visiting retail shops model will be more chance to be accepted to make final decision to this consumer habitually. What is this meaning to this consumer in these two different situation? I feel that the consumer will prefer to choose to buy the kind of product from online shopping if who is a excited person, so who can accept to use internet more than visiting retail shops , due to who enjoys to loneliness to sit down to use whose laptop to choose to buy any online products at home quiet environment. Otherwise, if the consumer does not like loneliness, who will like to leave whose home to visit retail shops to choose to buy any brands of products with whose friends or families in the noise shopping center environment, due to who will feel more happy and enjoyable to buy any products in the noise and social relationship with friends or family outside environment. It means that the product manufacturer needs to understand whether whose products can be more accepted to sell to its potential consumers from either online sale model or visiting retail shops traditional sale model as well as how to design its product styles to match its potential consumers to build positive emotion whether this product is suitable to sell from online sale channel. In general, the perceived case of use can influence perceived usefulness of the product, then to influence consumer's attitude to choose to buy the product. Hence, attitude can influence the consumer's commonly. I feel that the consumer will choose to visit retail shops to test the product's functions or attempt to touch the product or see the product's actual image in the retail shops, even who needs the salespeople to teach who how to use the product when feel the product is difficult to learn to use. Specially, it is a new innovative technological product, when it will be promoted to market to sell in the first time. Due to the consumer did not know this new product existed before, who needs the salespeople talk to whom to explain how to use this new technological innovative product to listen carefully. So, who will choose to visit retail shops to decide to buy this product with whose friends or families more than online shopping. Otherwise, if the consumer feels the product is ease to use and who like loneliness, who will accept to use internet to make final decision to choose online to buy the product in the quiet home environment more than traditional visiting retail shops model. It seems the external environment and the consumer's personality can influence the consumer's emotion to make final decision to choose to buy any brand of product. For example, the consumer feels the product is ease to learn to use or difficult to learn to use. It will influence the consumer choose to buy either from online or retail shops.

● How can internet cause positive emotion to consumers?

Online shopping lacks emotion physically experienced (e.g. examined, tried on, and used), it is difficultly for shoppers with little computer expertise, there are some general uncertainties associated in homes hopping of all kinds (e.g. concerns about product return, credit card security, loss of privacy, merchant legitimacy.) Each consumer's confidence might play an important role in predicting intentions to purchase. The factors influence whose confidence which may include, such as consumer's lower perceived risk, product appearance, image size and product movement were manipulated in context of simulated appeal web sites. Both manipulations in the computer medicated environment were expected to create virtual experiences affecting mood, perceived risk and purchase intent product image size is a significant factor. Product presentations using movement attract attention and generate good mood in on-line shoppers, even soft music listening in quiet home environment can influence consumer's emotion to cause online shopping intention. The benefits of online shopping in relation to traditional stores hopping are one of the driving forces in the adoption. Perceived usefulness has been used to explain consumer acceptance of online shopping. Perceived usefulness refers to the degree to which a person believes that using a particular system (e.g. an online shopping site) would enhance his or her job performance. Risk perception of online shopping can be risked into two predominant types behavioral risk and environment risk. Behavioral risk arises from online retailers who have a chance to behave in an opportunistic manner by taking advantage of the government's inability to monitor all transactions adequately. It includes product risks, psychology risks and seller performance risks. Environment risk is caused by the unpredictable nature of the purchasing medium-internet, which is beyond the control of online retailer and consumer. It includes financial risks and privacy risks. Perceived risk can be affected or moderated by a variety of factors, including consumer demographics, internet experience, product characteristics and attributes of a web site etc. The perceived product risk varies with the age and internet experience of consumers. As consumers get older, their accumulated experience and knowledge make their stopping more targeted of certain brands and make them more confident, which can reduce product risk and the need for conducting pre-product information searches. It is possible that in comparison to make consumers female consumers perceived the likelihood and consequences of negative outcomes as a result of purchasing online to be greater and their concerns regarding these verity of the consequences of privacy loss during online shopping were stronger. The effect of perceived risk may be subject to product characteristics. The risk is generally higher for high involvement products that require the problem solving behavior and have some degree of personal importance than for low involvement products. Hence, online retailers of low involvement products may have greater success in keeping buyers than those of high involvement products, if the former can provide on appealing shopping experience. Other attributes of products do matter to perceived risk . For example, the risk was perceived lower for product for categories associated with higher expenditure levels, more satisfying characteristics and feeling and touching before purchase. Consumer attitude is directly affected by users' belief about a system, which consist of perceived usefulness and once of use to use online to shopping in technology acceptance model to each individual consumer. In the technological acceptance model aspect view, it is possible that the consumer's perception of technology of safety and cost is important to influence who to choose to buy the product as well as self efficiency has been found to affect technology usage also through its effects on the emotional state of the user buy, for example, the manufacturer can reduce the consumer whose computer anxiety and it can increase behavioral control to its consumer more easily when its consumers enter it's product website to feel it is more safe to buy its products to compare to its online competitors' websites. Due to the characteristics of online retail context to innovative products, consumers are subjected to more influences in the virtual store where who are able to interact with an adaptive environment as a consequence on adaptive and interactive scenario is more appealing for consumers, with benefits for the decision making process. Thus, internet will influence consumers whose emotion to choose another online shopping model to any innovative products sale channel. Enjoyment can be considered the degree to which consumer perceives a certain technology as pleasant. It implies that richer technology leads to higher enjoyment for achieving a stronger influence on consumers' attitudes toward online retailers. I shall recommend any one innovative product manufacturer ought send questionnaires by to any individual consumer by email to enquire about such as below: (i) Do you feel this kind of innovative product is either easy or difficult more to learn to use ? It aims to predict their emotion to give feedback to let who to know whether consumers' emotion will be felt more easy or more difficult to use this product from these sample population. Then , this manufacturer can judge whether it ought to sell this kind of innovative product from either traditional retail shops or online shopping model. (ii) Do you feel you like to buy this product in either quiet environment or noise environment more? It aims to predict their positive emotion response to judge whether who accept to buy this kinds of innovative product in the quiet environment or noise environment more to decide to make visiting retail stores channel or online sale online to sell this product. (iii) Do you like to use internet advertisement or magazine advertisement channel to find this kind of product? It aims to predict internet online sale model or retail stores sale channel which is more acceptable to sell the manufacturer's products to attract to influence many customers to make final decision to buy its products more popular and acceptable. (iv) Do you need salespeople to talk to you to give truly products information to assist you to buy my brand of any products? .absolutely need .absolutely not need .may be need. may not be need. It aims to judge whether the online sale is more important sale channel or not to compare with retail shops sale channel. After it gathers these statistic information from these sample potential Consumers' email questionnaires, the manufacturer can analyze whether this kind of innovate product is more acceptable from online sale model or traditional retail shopping model in its country, even global sale. Thus, it can decide either to increase to open more retail shops or decrease retail shops numbers or concentrating on selling its products from online sale channel more sale methods.

Summary

Consumer emotion prediction can have many methods. However, I feel that these three methods are the most useful. Firstly, video camera recording technology can predict why the consumer chooses to buy the kind of product as well as face reading technology can measure whether what weights of the sugar ingredients to manufacture the weight of sweets, chocolate, soft drinks of the most good taste foods. Secondly, the manufacturer can concentrate on manufacturing whose new product which can own the most attractive attributable factor to attract which customers to choose to buy to reduce the invent lose risk. Thirdly, website sale channel must not be suitable to any manufacturers to choose to sell which products. If who can know whether their products are suitable to sell from internet or retail stores sale channel more. It can reduce the risk to loss their customers in long time. However, if you feel your product or food ought to sell from online channel. I recommend you ought need to do marketing research to evaluate whether which sale channel is the most suitable to research to sell your products or foods to persuade your clients to choose to buy. Otherwise, if your online sale channel is not suitable to sell to cause bad emotion to your clients. Thus, I believe it will reduce your client numbers due to you sell your products in the wrong sale channel.

CHAPTER THREE

Constructive consumer choice process predicts consumption method

● How constructive consumer choice process measures which attribute factor(s) can influence consumer chooses to buy any product or food in psychological view.

● Main Problem Being Addressed

The second aspect problem is judged whether constructive consumer choice is an important process to influence any consumer to choose to buy any products. If it is a real essential choice process, how product manufacturers can reduce their negative emotion is caused to choose not buy their products during this constructive process. The second aspect main problem is researched about consumer will choose to make final decision to buy the best choice of product from among brands of products . Hence, the constructive consumer choice process is a real essential choice process to any consumer generally, when individual consumer needs to compare different brands of products to choose to buy any product.

How product manufacturers can predict whose choice method to decide to prefer to make final decision to buy any products in the short days or the short time in the constructive consumer process. If manufacturers can know overall consumers' choice method, manufacturers will not design the not suitable style of products to manufacture to sell and who can know what the overall consumers' negative emotion is influenced who decide not to buy their products from their design style in order to manufacture more suitable style of product design . I shall recommend how manufacturers can predict consumer emotion in the constructive consumer choice process in psychological view.

My research is concerned knowledge opinion about how to predict consumer emotion whether what attribute factor(s)
are the most influence to the consumer to choose to buy the
manufacturer's product in whose process of choice. If manufacturer can early know whether what the most attractive attribute factor(s) are the most influence to the consumer to decide to buy whose product, so who can concentrate on manufacturing the different kinds of products to get the most influence attribute factor to attract consumers to choose to buy whose products. Hence, the manufacturer can know what reasons can cause the consumers who do not choose to buy its products during constructive consumer choice process generally , who can know how to improve its product's design method to concentrate on producing the most acceptable satisfactory level to sell to whose consumers in .Also I believe that the manufacturer can raise sale numbers if who know what bad factors to cause whose consumers choose not to buy whose products during the constructive consumer choice process. It can increase chance to change its product innovative strategy to raise confidence to judge what attributed factors are the important influence to cause consumers who either do not choose to buy or choose to buy its innovative products.

The attributable factor of any product may include some or all these factors. For example: Safety, durability, reasonable price, fashion, pretty design, loyalty, etc. different factors whether which attributed factor can cause the consumer feels positive emotion to prefer to choose to buy the manufacturer's innovative products. I shall recommend how to predict consumers' positive emotion to the manufacturer's products in the consumer's constructive choice process. However, the benefits to manufacturers if who can predict what attribute factors have much influence consumers to make final decision in the constructive consumer choice process. It includes as below:

● Concentrate on manufacturing the new products to predict which attribute factors are the importance existed to influence consumers' whose final decision to choose to buy the manufacturer's any kind of products in order to raise chance to increase sale numbers.

● To let consumers have more confidence to choose to buy the manufacturer's any products to use for long time.

● Avoiding to spend excess money and resources and time to concentrating on manufacturing the new product which own much of not important attribute factors to influence consumers to choose not to buy the manufacturer's products .

● Market review of constructive consumer process research limit

I feel that constructive consumer choice process can only be predicted to find whether what attributable factors can influence the consumer to choose to buy the manufacturer's product from shopping retail market only, but it can't not predicted from online shopping.

Because consumer needs to spend more time to compare different similar brands of product to find what the attributable factor(s) own(s) to the brand of product to attract who to make the final buying decision. If the consumer choose to buy the product, usually, who won't spend more time to gather the similar products' information to decide to which kind of product and who will buy the product from internet immediately. Otherwise, if the consumer choose leave home to walk to different shops to choose to buy the kind of product, who have more time to spend to different shops to compare the different brand products to make final buying decision. Hence , constructive consumer choice process will only occur at visiting shops' consumption to any individual or group consumption.

● Related Background of constructive consumer process

May constructive consumer choice process is a psychological factor to influence consumers' emotion to make final decision to buy either kind of emotion product or rational product in consumption market generally. How can product manufacturers detect consumers' emotion to judge whether their products are belonged to be more kind of emotion product or rational product during they decide to sell different kind of products or foods to consumers?

Constructive consumer choice is an important process to influence any consumers to choose to buy any products. I shall give my idea to indicate how product manufacturers can predict whether their products are belonged to be either more kind of emotional product or more kind of rational product at different suitation. It aims to reduce their negative emotion is caused to choose not buy their products from their constructive consumer choice process.

Consumer decision making trends technological change and information explosion nowadays. Generally, consumers need to compare different brands of products from their characteristics , such as quality, fashion, design style, colors, prices, functions etc. factors to decide which is the most valuable choice to buy among of these different kinds of similar products from global consumption channel, such as electronic internet shopping channel or traditional retail shopping channel of two kinds of sale methods. Due to consumers can get any kinds of products' the most updated information from internet, television , magazines etc. advertisement channel at home conveniently. Thus, it causes nowadays consumers will concern to use a variety of strategic contingent on their consumption to demand to choose to buy what is the most valuable product considerately.

After consumers spend much time to make constructive choice, who will make final decision to choose to buy which kind of product is the most valuable from their positive emotion. In general, before any consumer chooses to make decision to buy any product, whose option is in a choice it will be assumed to have a utility or subjective value feeling to the product that it depends only on the option. Finally, it is assumed that the consumer has ability of skill in a computation that enables the calculation of which option will maximize whose received value and selects accordingly.

Why are preferences constructive logic buying decision in constructive consumer choice is important? One reason individuals may construct preferences is that who lacks the cognitive resources to generate well preferences for many situations. A second important reason is that consumers often multiple goals to be given decision problem. It implies preferences constructive choice will influence any consumer to change whose emotion to prefer to buy the product among of the same kind of target products. However, the fact that a choice is contingent need not simply that the processing was constructive , that is developed on the spot. A food or soft drink can be either a rational product or emotional product. For example, a consumer may have a well established, but contingent, preference for have chocolate on a cold day and a cold soft drink on a warm day, such a preference is not constructive to influence the consumer's emotion to spend long time to compare other similar foods or drinks to make the final decision to choose to buy the chocolate or a cold soft drink among of the other similar kind of target foods or drinks in supermarket. In this situation, it seems that the chocolate and soft drink is emotional product. A major purpose , therefore is to provide a conceptual framework for understanding constructive consumer choice how to influence consumers' emotion to make final consumption decision in the rational environment only. This framework then allows to accomplish the two major goals:

(i) Reviewing consumer decision research with the framework serving as a organizing device and (ii) Using this review to gaps in my knowledge that suggest new research directions to predict consumer's individual emotion of purchasing behavior. In general, in consumer view point, consumer product motive can provide two kinds of motives . One kind is emotional product motive which persuades the consumer on the basic of whose emotion, the buyer doesn't try to reason out or typically analysis the need for purchase. Another kind is rational product motive which arises on the basic of logical analysis and proper evaluation, the buyer makes rational decision after chief evaluation of the purpose, alternatives available, cost benefit and such valid reasons.

How to predict consumer decision tasks and decision strategies? In some cases, the two options may be simply to either accept or reject an alternative. The attributes may vary in consumers' potential consequences, the product desirability to the consumer and the consumer's acceptance to make off less of one attribute for more of another. For example, a consumer may fairly certain about the values of some of the attributes. (e.g. reliability, safety factors) to the product to influence the consumer's buying decisions. For example, a consumer considers the cars to decide that safety was the most important attribute, processed only that attribute with the best value on that attribute limited effectively requires selective attention to information or a consumer might engage in attribute processing by examining the price of each of the cars. Including that car (B) was the most expensive, car (A) was the least expensive, and that (C) had a very good price. However, the consumer could process in an alternative based fashion by examining the reliability, price, safety of car (A) in order to form a overall valuation of the car. In compensatory strategy, a good value on one attribute can't make up for a poor value on another. If a consumer decide to choose the safest car, then car(D) will be chosen regardless of as high price and regardless of the high ratings for car (B) on reliability or car (E) for fashion.

● Consumer decision strategies

First step, the amount of information processed. For example, an automobile choice is as implied by most rational choice models to consider each of the available cars or it may only a consideration of a limited set of information. (e.g. repeating what one choice last time). Second step, different amount, information can be processed for each attribute or alternative (selecting processing) or same amount of information can be processed each attribute or alternative. Third step, the pattern of processing (whether by alternative (brand) or by attribute. Final step, the consumer will select to buy the product, based on whether the strategy is compensatory or non compensatory.

In addition, aspects of the environment the capture involuntary attention may set in motion and consumer behavioral responses. (e.g. in a loud environment is as a threat to cause the consumer's negative emotion to decide to buy the product). It implies quiet environment has more positive influence to consumer's individual emotion. For many consumer choice, there is little emotion involvement or need to justify. The choice goals and the extent to which different strategies accomplish these goals in different task environment. For example, proposed measured of cognitive effort and accuracy. With respect to cognitive effort, any decision strategy can be decomposed into more elementary information processes, such as reading on item of information, comparing two items of information, eliminating items of information and so on for a general decision to analyze information processing for each individual consumer when who need to choose to buy any products. For another example, a consumer can conceptualize to read the value for each attribute weight, comparing the weight just read with the largest weight found previously until the most important attributable has been found and then reading the values for the options on that attribute and comparing the until the largest value is found. It weight adding strategy could be thought as reading weights and values, multiplying the two ,moving on to the next weight and value and multiplying them, adding the product. Consumer sometimes face emotion choice. Such choices arise when there are choice conflicts between goals that are very important to the individual. (e.g. one can't attain all goals given the set of available options and must give up something on one important goal to attain more of another important goal). Examples of such emotion consumer choices include trading off the safety of an automobile against environmental concerns (if larger vehicles fare better in crashes but worse in gas mileage) or trading health risks due to the presence of insects in one's house versus health risks from having chemicals sprayed in one's yard. Such choice can easily lead to negative emotion, since the trade-offs required represent threats to the attainment of importance or valued goals. The degree of emotion often depends on the values of the options. (e.g. the degree of conflict and which specific attributes are involved in the conflict). However, the negative emotion is caused by the consumer's choice process, it is not only caused by external environment, e.g. noise influence. Choice processes under negative emotion may therefore be affected by accuracy and effort concerns as modified by emotion minimization concerns. In particular, two general copying strategies may apply in consumer emotion situations: problem focuses copying (direct actions aimed at improving the person environment relationship to influence the consumer's emotion), and emotion focused copying (indirect actions aimed at minimizing emotion through changes in the amount or content of thought about the situation). Hence, manufacture will expect that increased negative emotion due to the choice situation will lead to more extensive processing. New products were evaluated more favorably when their attributes were moderate only when consumers had limited knowledge about the product category. Consumers had more extensive knowledge about the category , their evaluations were influenced by associations to specific attributes based on their final choice level. Thus, knowing what the consumer's the most need of attributes of the product is very important in whose construct choice process. The affective tests consumer emotion's prediction weakness. The primary purpose of affective tests is to assess the personal response (preference or acceptance) of current or potential customers to a product idea or a specific product characteristics. Qualitative affective tests are those (e.g. interviews and focus groups) that measure subjective response of a sample of consumers to the sample kinds of products by having those consumers talk about their feelings in an interview or small group setting. A highly trained interviewer/ moderator is required because of the high level of interaction between the interviewer/moderator and the consumers. Types of qualitative affective tests include focus groups, focus panels, mini-group and one-on-one interviews. However, qualitative affective tests will have these problems, such as with focus groups, individual answer can get lost in the group conversation. In addition, individual can reject from expressing opinions contrary to the group because of perceived peer pressure or group think. Panels which are focus group that meet repeated suffer from the same problems as focus groups. With one-on-one interview fasters might substantially temper a negative assessment of a product in order to not to appear honest answer or because they like the interviewer and don't want to hurt their feelings.

● Internet questionnaires recommendation
I recommend any individual company can send internet questionnaires to individual to detect what attribute factors can influence individual consumer's emotion to make the final consumption decision to choose to

buy its innovative new products by email before their new products will be manufactured. Thus, the manufacturer can predict whether what attribute factor can be the most potential influence to individual's emotion to choose to buy whose new products generally. For example, one car manufacturer can send email questionnaires to individual consumer to invite who to fill its questionnaires in its website, these questionnaire questions can indicate as below: (a) What attribute factor(s) can influence you to choose to buy our company's new design style sport car products?. reliability .new fashion .fast speed .brand .popular. reasonable price . durability, .safety .more functions . unique design style (b) Which factor do you feel which is the most important to influence you to make the final buying decision to choose to buy our company's new design style sport car products ?

In general, this company's all sport cars which are rational products. It means any consumer will prefer to spend time to compare its any style of sport cars to other brands of sport cars to make final decision to choose to buy which brand of sport car. For example, if one consumer feels safety attribute factor is the most important to influence who chooses to buy any sport cars. Then, he/she will demand to attempt to drive to detect this car company's any style of sport cars to test whether which can satisfy to whose safe demand. Even, if who feel other brands' style of sport cars can satisfy whose safe demand, he/she will be possible to attempt to drive to detect other brands of similar style sports cars to compare to this brand of sport car to make final purchase decision. Owing to there are many brands of sport cars which are provided to individual consumer to compare to choose to make final decision to buy in any country. It seems that any consumer will prefer to spend time to make logical and rational analysis to compare them and who won't be influenced by whose emotion to decide to buy any brands of sport cars in the short time easily. Thus sport cars is belonged to rational product more then emotional product. As this reason, so I recommend this sport car company needs to prepare email questionnaires to enquire its potential individual consumer to attempt to let who to give feedback to predict whether what attribute factors can influence whose emotion to choose to buy its any kind style sport cars as well as whether what attribute factor will be the most importance to compare the other attribute factors to make final cause to influence final decision to choose to buy its any sport cars to avoid the worst attribute factor is caused. Following the car company gathers different feedback to predict whether what attribute factors are as well as what the worst factor is from these

sample potential consumer's idea of its email questionnaire. Then, it can predict the result from consumers' idea to make final decision whether which are the least attractive attribute factors which will influenced any individual consumer to decide not to buy its any style of sport cars. It aims to predict whether what are the least attractive attribute factors to cause bad emotion to the consumer to choose not to buy the kind of sport car generally. Such as, not reliable engines, old fashion , slow speed, unpopular brand, not reasonable price, not durability, not safety, less functions or not unique design style of whether which are the least attractive attribute factors. Hence, it can predict whether which attribute factors will be the attractive influence to cause its any potential consumer to choose to buy its any new innovative sport cars in order to concentrate on manufacturing any new innovative style sport cars to design which must own the most attractive attribute factors before it decides to manufacture its new style of sport cars. In conclusion, it seems that constructive consumer choice is an important process to influence any consumer to choose to buy any products. I recommend any company ought attempt to prepare questionnaires to investigate whether which the most attractive attribute factors are and which the least attractive attribute factors are influenced to each potential consumer will choose to buy or not buy to its launch innovative new products by email questionnaire channel. In general, youth people will feel ease to use online to shopping to compare to old people. I shall indicate online car brands comparison Constructive consumer choice processes Table 1 An example of a consumer decision task
car reliability price safety speed
A worst best good very poor
   B best worst worst good

C poor very good average average

D average poor best worst
   E worse very good good best
Attributes are scored on seven point scales ranging from best to worst, with indicating the most desirable value for the attribute and worst indicating the least desirable value.

CHAPTER FOUR

Ethnographic research psychological consumer emotion

How can ethnographic research predict consumer emotion ?

Critically assess the role of ethnographic research as a means of learning More about buyer behavior. To critically assess whether the role of ethnographic research as a means of learning more about buyer behavior. I shall indicate what the marketers who use general methods to learn more about buyer behavior to compare to ethnographic research difference. In general, marketers learn buyer behavior who shall follow the simplified stages in the buyer decision process , such as the beginning is from need recognition to information search to evaluate to decision to the end of post purchase evaluation stage. Hence, the any buyers behavior shall be cycle stage to decide whether who shall repeat to choose to buy the company's product or use it's service if who feel the product or service had achieved their satisfaction after who spent. The marketers shall use questionnaires or marketing researches to enquire consumers to gather their ideas to analysis to get evaluation to assess whether how whose companies need to produce what kinds of new products style, design, color, price level and sale channels to achieve the most suitable marketing strategy to raise their sale competition. Otherwise, the role of ethnographic search is one different method to learn more about buyer behavior. In general, companies shall not need to arrange questionnaires to enquire participants to fill to answer questions to gather data to carry on evaluation and which do not need to follow the simplified stages to assess target client groups purchase decision process to carry on the sale and post purchase evaluation cycle to evaluate whether what are their product criteria or weaknesses which need to improve to raise their sale competition in their market. I think ethnographic research can get closer to the truth about consumer behavior. On behalf of companies' clients, which can seek to uncover hidden truths about the way their clients' lead their lives, by paying volunteers to be followed for days on end, being filmed and having their every more recorded. Companies will pay their target householder participant group to carry on an observational survey by digital cameras to be filmed record at home. One essential feature of ethnographic research is that it must not have any predetermined agenda.

There is little value in undertaking this type of research if the mind set of the researcher is expecting to see preconceived phenomena, it is the unexpected that is often of most interest, and which is so difficult to pick up through more structured forms of survey. In fact, participants in a survey may feel self conscious when who are being filmed, and the more interesting insights are likely to be observed when participants are feeling relaxed and off their guard .It is not just what people actually do that can be interesting, but what they almost do, and the body language used when members of the household are discussing an issue. It can take several hours of filming to yield just a few moments of true insights into participants' true attitudes and behavior.

One example of the company's ethnographic research in action was provided by a project commissioned by the footwear brand Dr Martens. It wanted to understand how young people used fashion brands in their every lives . Why for example, did some brands, such as Nike trainers or baseball caps become popular in youth culture? The researchers identified groups of young people around the world who responded to Dr Martens' target market. In return for a payment, volunteers were followed for several days and their daily routines filmed with a handheld digital camera. In total, 180 hours of captured film was edited to just one hour of highlights showing the key drivers of youth culture which are relevant to the Dr Martens brand. It seemed that young people preferred fashions that allowed them to customize an item of clothing and in some way take ownership of it. The research drew the conclusion that iconic fashion items for young people had to have a distinctive label or style that made their wearers stand out as part of a tribe. Hence, ethnographic research seems to help this company to know why the young clients choose to buy other brand sport shoes, it is possible that they the other brands sport shoes' color or design can be accepted more to than to buy Dr Marten brand's sport shoes when they wear different style of clothing. Hence, it can use digital camera to observe the worldwide choice of paying target youth volunteers whose daily individual behaviors at homes to get the more actual evidence to evaluate what factors influence youth clients choose to buy other brands of sport shoes. Otherwise, if it use structured questionnaire surveys to enquire youth clients , it is possible that who can not give their feedbacks honestly. Otherwise, observable youth people whose daily activities can help this company to know it is possible that their design and color of clothing are one factor to influence their choice to buy preferable brands of sport shoes to wear if who felt the brand of sport shoe was suitable to wear to influence their clothing to be felt more smart in appearance. However, I suggest companies to avoid to tell householders what the research project is about, until it is over. That way, the chances of participants deliberately playing to the camera can be reduced.

Hence, ethnographic researcher ought not tell to participants why who needs to record their daily activities at home till to the end of observable survey finishing due to it is possible that the participants will not perform their actual behaviors if who knew the researcher's observable intention. However, if marketers need to understand how whose companies clients actually make purchase decisions to their products, who shall use structured questionnaire surveys for collecting large scale factual data, but it will have major weaknesses when companies can not understand individual's attitude. Complex sets of factors that influence their buying decisions can only rarely be captured by a questionnaire.

Qualitative approaches such as those using focus groups can get closer to the truth, but participants often still find themselves inhibited from telling the full story to the companies to know.

Ethnography is one of many approaches that can be found within social research. Ethnography was a descriptive account of a community or culture. Ethnography usually involves the researcher participating in people's daily lives for an extended

period of time, watching what happens, listening to what is said, and/ or asking questions through informal and formal interviews collecting documents. In more detailed terms, ethnographic work usually has most of the following features: People actions are studied in every contexts rather than under conditions created by the researcher, such as in experimental setups or highly structured interview situations as well as data are gathered from a range of sources including documentary evidence of various kinds, but participant observation and/or relatively informal conversations are usually the main ones as well as data collection is for the most past relatively unstructured in two senses and it doesn't involve following through detailed research design at the start and the categories that are used for interpreting what people say or do are not built into the data collection process through the use of observation schedules or questionnaire to analysis.

Generally, fairly small scale, perhaps a single setting or group of people. This is a facilitate in depth study and the analysis of data involves interpretation of the meanings, functions and consequences of human actions and how these are implicated in local and perhaps also wider contexts what are produced for the most part are verbal descriptions, explanations and theories and statistical analysis play a subordinate role at most. How ethnography can learn more about buyer behavior. It means collection of data to pursue an answers to these questions more effectively and to test these against evidence. Collecting data in natural settings, in other words in those that have not been specially set up for research purposes (such as experiments or formal interviews). Where participant observation is involved the researcher must have some role in the studied and this

will usually have to be done at least through implicit and probably also through explicit, negotiation with people.

The methodological model for social research is physical science conceived in terms of the logic of the experiment. Ethnography was sometimes dismissed as quite inappropriate to social science on the grounds that the data and findings it produces are subjective. Hence, ethnographic research is the role to learn more about buyer behavior through marketers may have been listening more to consumers (e.g. through qualitative research), efforts have almost always been directed at controlling consumers; ranges of products or services pre determined by producers have been pushed through with little real involvement of consumers in the process at a time in which consumers are ever more aware of what is being done to marketers. Ethnographic field research involves the study of groups and people as who go about every day lives. There has two distinct activities. First, the ethnographer enter into a social setting and gets to know the people involved in it; who participates in the daily routines; develops ongoing relations with the people in it and observes all the approach. But second the ethnographer writes down in regular systematic ways what who observes and learns when participating in the daily rounds of life of others. Thus, the researcher creates an accumulating written record of these observations and experiences. These two interconnected activities comprise the core of ethnographic search: firsthand participation in some initially unfamiliar social world and the production of written accounts of that world by drawing upon such participation. Hence, ethnographers are committed to get close to the activities and everyday people.

Getting close minimally requires physical and social proximity to the daily rounds of people's lives and activities, the field researcher must be able to take up positions in the midst of the key sites and scenes of other's lives in order observe and understand whom. In learning about others through active participation in their lives and activities. Finally, close continuing participation in the lives of others encourages appreciation of social life as ongoing processes. Through participation the field researcher sees how people do uncertainty and confusion, how meaning is through talk and collective action, how understandings change over time.

Consumer behavior refers to the behavior that consumers display in searching for purchasing, using, evaluating and disposing of products and services that who expect will satisfy their needs and it's behaviors that are directly involved in the action of obtaining, consuming and spending products/services, including the decision processes that precede and follow these actions. The knowledge of consumer behavior helps the marketer to understand how consumer think, feel and select from alternative like products, brands and the like and how the consumers' buying behaviors are influenced by their environment, the reference groups, family and salespersons. Most of the factors are uncontrollable and beyond the controls of marketers, but who have to be considered when trying to understand the complex behavior of the consumers. Consumers buying cycle processes involved when individuals or groups select, purchase, use or dispose of products or services or ideas or experiences to satisfy needs and desires.

In the marketing context, the term consumer refers not only to the act of purchase itself, but also to patterns of aggregate buying which include pre-purchase and post purchase activities.

Pre-purchase activity might consist of the growing awareness of a need or wants and a search for and evaluate of information about the products and brands that might satisfy it. Post purchase activities include the evaluation of the purchased item in use and the reduction of any anxiety which accompanies the purchase of expensive and infrequently bought items. The various factors include lifestyles and its impact on the consumer behavior. On the first hand, ethnographic research can learn more about buyer behavior as below: ethnographic research described the dominant, positivistic consumer perspectives and methodological and analytical overview of the traditional perspectives. There are two factors mainly influencing the consumers for decision making. Risk aversion and innovativeness. Risk aversion is a measure of how much consumers need to be certain and sure of what who are purchasing. Highly risk adverse consumers need to be very certain about what who are buying. Whereas less risk adverse consumers on tolerate some risk and uncertainty in their purchasing. The second variable, innovativeness is a global measure which captures the degree to which consumers are willing to take chances and experiment with new ways of doing things. Hence, ethnographic research can learn whether the buyer's shopping motivation is abound with which various measures of individual characteristics, e.g. innovative, variety seeking etc. different factors to the buyer behavior.

On the second hand, perception is a mental process, whereby an individual selects data or information from the environment organizes it and then draws significance or meaning from it. Perceived fit is an attitudinal measure of how appropriate a certain channel of distribution is for a specific product. Consumer's perception of the fit between a service/ product and channel is very influential in determining whether who will consider using that channel for a specific service. In fact, perceived fit was found to be more important than consumer's preference for the distribution method or service. Product quality and packaging and brand awareness familiarity with a channel is a measure of the general experience who have with purchasing products through special channels , e.g. internets, newspapers advertisement factors let consumers to decide to choose to buy or not buy the specific product. Shopping motives are defined as consumer's wants and needs as who relate to outlets at which to shop. Two groups of motives, functions and non functional have been proposed with time, place and possession needs and refer to rational aspects of
channel choice. The functional motives included convenience, price comparison. Otherwise, the non functional motives entailed recreation and it related to social and emotional reasons. Hence, ethnographic research can assess whether the product or service is the functional motive or non functional motive to cause the buyer's choice.

On the third hand, economic theory holds that of largely rational and conscious economic calculations. Thus, the individual buyer seeks to spend whose income on those products that will deliver the most utility (

satisfaction) according to his tastes and relative prices. It aimed to simplify assumptions and examine the effects of changes in single variables (e.g. price) holding all other variables constant. (e.g. low price of product is the higher the sales. The identified the impact of price differentials on consumers' brand preferences; changes in produces on demand variations; changes in price on demand sensitivity and scarcity on consumer choice behavior amongst many others. The consumer behavioral perspective in contrast to the economic view which underscores the importance of internal processes in consumer decision making, the behavioral perspective emphasizes the role of external environmental factors in the process of learning, when which it is argued causes behavior. The behavioral perspective therefore focuses on external environmental, such as advertisement that stimulate consumer response through learning. Consumers must be exposed to information, e.g. advertisement of it is to influence their behavior. Hence, ethnographic research can assess whether the product/service is consumer behavioral perspective or behavioral perspective to cause the buyer's choice.

On the fourth hand, consumers were suggest that high involvement with a product results in an extended problem followed by an information search, alternative evaluation, purchase and post purchase activities. The process is aided by an active information processing sequence involving exposure, attention, comprehension, acceptance and retention. The choice is determined by the outcome of the information process aided decision sequence may have satisfying or dissatisfying outcomes. Consumer's motivation and intention and that unpredictable factors (such as non availability brand or insufficient funds) may result in modification of the actual choice made by a consumer. This model assumes that observed consumer behavior is preceded by intrapersonal psychological states and events (attitude intention-purchase sequence). Hence, the events are as outputs of the processing of information, taking for granted that consumers seek and use information as part of their rational problem solving and decision making processes. Hence, ethnographic research can learn why the buyer doesn't choose to buy the product whether it is unpredictable or predictable psychological factors.

On the fifth hand, personality perspective means some purchases have more personal relevance than others. When this partly reflects on factors, such as price, it also bears on the way in which some products enhance the consumer's self concept , e.g. possessions are considered to reflect on a consumer's image of whom. Personality in general is understood as a concept. Personality has also been understood as the unique way in which traits, attitudes, when individuals might not always be uniform and predictable in their patterns of choice in different situations, it might be possible to make sense of and to forecast the general reactions of broadly defined groups and classes of purchasers.

It is the concept of consumer general behavioral response patterns that forms the basis for marketing's personality based segmentation strategies. The possibility of using measures of personality to guide marketing action, for example in segmenting markets , tailoring new brands of innovative consumers and repositioning mature brands has encouraged a large volume of research. Attitude itself is a learning experience and can lead to a change in attitudes before buyers enter the buying process. Thus, attitudes don't automatically guarantee all types of behavior. They are really the product of social forces interacting with the individual's unique temperament and abilities and social influences are not all of the behavioral variations in people. Two individuals subject to the same influences are not likely to have identical attitudes, although those attitudes will probably more points than those of two and cognition. Affect refers to the way a consumer feel about an attitude object, behavior involves the person's intentions to do something with regard to an attitude object and finally cognition refers to the beliefs a consumer has about an attitude object.

Thus, ethnographic research can learn whether it is from external social factors more or internal personality factors more to cause the buyer's choice. The theory of cognitive information processing , attitudes are formed in the order of beliefs, affect and behavior. Attitudes based on behavioral learning follow the beliefs, behaviors and affect sequence and finally attitudes formed based on the experiential hierarchy follow the affect, behavior and beliefs route. A consumer who is highly involved with a product / service category and who perceives a high level of product/ service differentiation between alternatives will follow the cognitive hierarchy (beliefs affect behavior). From the ethnographic research marketers perspective the sequence of attitude formation is from a communication point of views from a strategic point of view, such as it has proved useful in specifying the different elements that work together to influence buyers' evaluations of attitudes ; products or services may be composed of many attributes or qualities, some of which may be more important than others to particular people. So consumer's decision is to act on whose attitude is affected by other factors, such as whether it is felt other factors, such as whether it is felt that buying a product/ service would be met with approval by friends and family. The complexity of attitudes is underscored by multi attribute attitude models, in which sets of beliefs and evaluations are identified and combined to predict an overall attitude.

On the final hand, the situational influence perspective, a situation is defined by factors over and above the characteristics of a person and product or service. For example, situational affects may be behavioral (e.g. entertaining friends), experiential or perceptual (e.g. being depressed or being pressed for time). According to the behavioral influence perspective of low involvement decision situation, consumer decision making is a learned response to environmental cues, as when a person decided to buy something on impulse that is prompted as a surprise special in a store.

According to this approach, then ethnographic research marketers must concentrate on assessing the characteristics of the environment, such as the physical surroundings and product/service placement, that influence members of that target market. For example, point of purchase (such as product/ service samples) are particularly useful in inducing impulse purchases. Ethnographic research marketers focus on measuring consumers' effective responses to products or services and develop offerings that elicit appropriate subjective reactions and employ effective symbolism. Situational effects can also be perceptive, e.g. there could be a number of ways in which mood can influence purchase decisions. For example, stress can impact information processing and problem solving abilities. In addition, time poverty can impact buying decisions. An individual's priorities determine whose time style. According, consumer buying change is not something which consumers do for themselves, rather it is a result of something that is done to them by some internal ,e.g. trait or external ,e.g. environment force over which they have little or no control. Thus, ethnographic research can assess what is the situational influence factors to cause the buyer to choose to buy the product or consume the service. In conclusion, conditions of competition are changing rapidly today and companies need strategies to react to those changes promptly to raise competition. Due to technological developments, physical differences of products/ services have decreased. Differentiation should be on the meanings products/
services bear instead of on their physical features and a successful brand differentiation can be possible by building personality. Hence,

understanding consumer behaviors are related to marketing natures in the product sale or service provision to every marketer who needs to considerate to win whose competitors.

2. Discuss the ethical issues that are raised by ethnographic research.

Consumer research has been important to the development of marketing theory and practice. Consumers are seldom, if ever, involved in the research design and analysis processes which raises issues that go beyond ethics. Particularly, problematic when participant observation is employed , as little is and little could be addressed by research guidelines and codes of ethics relevant to marketing research. Some of the relevant ethical issues to participant observation that arise from the lack of the consumer in the research process as well as the potential issues that may be involved in participatory research designs, the shortcomings of the available ethnographic marketing research guidelines and codes of ethics as for as participant observation is concerned. Some argument regards the real time and nature of ethical circumstances at the field where the ethnographic researcher must often respond to unexpected situations immediately.

3. Why ethical ways of thinking it is important to recognize that are raised by ethnographic research.

It is possible that the issues of power that can arise ethnographic research as well as it is from the consequences of simply doing
research , even if the intentions are good and it is from the fact that ethnographic research marketers' knowledge system is necessarily linked to other forms of structural power (e.g. gender, race, development, the system). The ethnographic research marketers whose emotional and power issues present in ethnographic research relationships are also acknowledged to influence ethnographic results, and this is where the key issues of using research participants for data collection comes in. Ethnographic research designs that objectify and don't include research participants in the conceptualization of the research study through to data analysis have been widely criticized by ethnographic researchers and these issues must be considered within the scope of the ethics of care.

Researchers (ethnographers) need have moral responsibilities toward research, included informed consent, confidentiality, reliability and validity. In sum, ethical guidelines and codes of conduct can be beneficial in alerting consumer researchers of ethical ways of conducting research. However, participants needed rules to be aided by researchers' own ethical reasoning in the field. The ethnographic researchers need to highlight the importance of constant negotiation of participation in the different stages of research, how participants may not be willing (due to lack of time or even personal circumstances) to help ethnographic researchers in the data analysis process and how researchers' own deadlines and academic constraints may get in the way of the idealized research process of involvement between ethnographic research participants and researchers are well to their discussed topic. In general, ethnographic researchers need to know what who need to understand about ethics, such as harm, consent, data protection etc. recap of ethical approval what it is and what ethnographic researchers need to do and what further sources of information and support need.

In ethic principles, ethnographic research should be designed, reviewed and undertaken to ensure integrity and quality. Participants must normally be informed fully about the purpose, methods and intends possible uses of research, what their participation entails and what risks, the confidentiality must be respected research participants must take part voluntarily, harm to research participants must be avoided in all instances and the independence of research must be clear and any conflicts to interest or partiality must be explicit and increasing stakeholder demands. The mature of the ethical consumer is educated, middle class or over emotional to decide what kind products who needs to buy and how many numbers are enough to buy. For example, with the environment dropping out of media attention, ethic provided new moral ground and campaigns or opening of a chain of ethical supermarkets, ethical image became a desirable commodity for the big retailers. Some ethical customers need to satisfy with fair trade marked products to buy from the ethical supermarkets. How morality may play a significant role in the performance of buyers' actions. It is concerned specifically with how rules, responsibilities and values centering on right or wrong influence the character of consumption. The idea that morality (ethicality) can have a considerable impact upon the consumption. Hence, I think business moral performance is needed to satisfy every buyer's decision of consumption and it is linked to the ethnographic research growing literature on ethical consumer behavior. Within psychology, for instance, morality can be seen as a process of cognitive learning where systematic punishment and reward help to educate individuals of their actions. Whether consumption is informed by at least some of the available moral perspectives to some of the available moral perspectives, so it caused ethical issues that are raised by ethnographic research. Ethical consumption is concerned with predicting market behavior, it included some kind of relationship between the attitudes, values and behaviors of a defined ethical consumer group. For example, ethnographic researchers have been interested in the effects of environmental concern on environmentally friendly consumer behavior. Depending on how ethical consumption is defined, it recognizes alternative forms of what are essentially moral values, attitudes and buyer individual behavior. Consumer behavior has been changed by external elements, such as economy, technology, cultures, religion etc. factors. It would be unfortunate to be great importance for an understanding of ethical consumption issues.

In conclusion, consumption behavior is the art of need for desire to, it could be thought of as directly influenced by certain core values held as sacred within society. For example, ethical buyer behavior may concerns about animal protection, environmental protection, human protection etc. life rights issue. Facts, knowledge and truth about morality in consumption are seen as being raised by ethnographic research. According, the relationship between morality and consumers behavior could be better through of as the products of a continued process of political, social, technological and religious re-organization of life. For example, capabilities of new digital , microchip technology enhanced many consumers with the delights of efficient, task-saving, small and shiny products. Simultaneously, and not unrelated turbo-charges cars, mobile phones, cock tail parties etc. high technological products are arguably reflected power, success and good living to influence buyer behavior ethically daily in our society. Hence, I believe ethical issues that are needed to consider by ethnographic research.

4. Discuss possible alternative approaches by which marketers may learn more about youth culture.

Market based trading -selling, buying and consuming has existed in our society. Human action and interaction and behaving in different roles in exchange markets and various trading situations which is a typical of consumers and market trading interplays of several actors in economic, societal and cultural contexts as well as consumer behavior and consumer culture and consumption which have close relationship. Individual youth consumer or a group of youth consumers who is described as humanistic economics where people, their values and culture are primarily analyzed. In general, research on brands and organizational issues of the marketing function defined the questions of how to sell more products or provide more services to speed up the general level of consumption in order to better the economic situation of a firm or a nation. Basically, individual youth buyer seeks to speed whose income on those products/services what will deliver the most utility, typically satisfaction, according to whose tastes and budget. In economic, consumer behavior is identified with rational decision making. Decisions are automatically translated into purchasing and consuming, The price and income constraints are generally accepted factors in an economic analysis of

consumer behavior. Consequently, consumers are seen as rational actors that purposefully optimize the production of their utility.

Sociological and macro and cultural perspective which focuses on consuming , emphasizes on emotions, multicultural new consumers aspects, cultural studies and the meaning of culture for consumer research surfaced also in the late 1980 years. For example, consumption symbolism, different aspects to property and possessions, political consumption, research and cultures and subcultures. In consumer studies can be traced to the mid 1990 years, when consumer culture was recognized as a distinct cultural entity. Consumption was seen as a society activity which above all others, unities economy and culture. The one alternative approach is that learning more about youth culture, there is a clear common sense about its influence on social youth consumption changes, and the importance of its analysis in order to understand modern youth consumption. For example, marketers may learn more how to make youth to cause excessive consumption nowadays. The influence of the means of mass communication and oriented medias has contributed to send promotion messages to different youth audiences, e.g. from children and teen ages to youths. To see themselves in real conditions why who need to buy products or need services before beyond their possibilities have been planned to buy electronics, cars and even a house etc. products.

The another alternative approach is that marketers may also learn what are youth consumer modern culture how to make them, such as symbol status and power how become habituated to consume familiar products/ services able to reinforce familiar image in youth cultural different target groups. The final alternative approach is that culture is sociological influence on client's needs, it is based on the individual's physiological and psychological needs, such as food choice. Maslow recognized that once individual have satisfied these basic physiological needs, such as foods and drinks, who may seek to satisfy social needs by cultural influence, for example, the need to have meaningful interaction with peers. More complex still, western cultures see increasing numbers of people seeking to satisfy essentially internal needs for self satisfaction, products therefore satisfy increasing complex needs. Moreover, food is no longer seen as a basic necessary to be purchased and cooked for self consumption with growing prosperity, youth people have sought to satisfy social needs by eating out with friend or family. Youth peoples' satisfaction of such social needs may influences on their foods sating basic needs. Hence, if the youth clients had afford to go to restaurant to eat more expensive and good taste foods. The high class food culture can change the youth client's food necessity to influence whose food choice. A young child is often considered society unacceptable, so such youth behavior is socialized out before the child reaches adulthood. The faculty cultural influences a child's perception of the world and the family cultural influences lasts into adulthood. For example of this effect on buying processes can be found in youth adults selection of a particular brand breakfast cereal because it is the one that who were brought up with youth individuals are surrounded by peer group/or reference groups with act as a guide for youth consumption of behavior peer groups can be primary and direct to influence their youth culture (e.g. colleagues at work and school), popular movie actors can secondary and indirect to influence to their youth culture (e.g. guideline or behavior provided by popular movie actors or media figures) ; youth individuals culture can also

identify with a social class and the values of this class can influence youth behavior, e.g. school culture or working class. However, culture in its widest sense influences youth buying behavior and deference to suppliers can differ significantly between different countries' youth culture to choose to sell their products or provide their services to the countries' youth markets. Youth needs are also influenced by the situation in which youth currently find themselves in their countries. The subjects of age and socio-economic status can have profound effects on youth buying behavior at different youth age market segmentation, such as youth client groups can divided to any companies to concentrate on selling, e.g. between 20 ages to 40 ages or between 10 ages to 20 ages etc. different age groups.

In conclusion, marketer may learn more about youth culture from different countries' family life cycle stages of change which have sought to take account of their increasing complexity to influence to estimate the countries' youth buyer numbers. The family relationships can include single parent family, married parent family, no children family youth buyer groups of family life cycle youth buyer changing numbers in marketers' target countries. Due to all different countries family life cycle youth buyer numbers can indicate the countries' youth individual needs changing numbers and the target countries' youth buyer numbers are likely to change their purchase tastes and needs as youth culture goes through life. Hence, marketers can measure the target countries youth age segmentation estimate numbers to decide how many products or how much services to supply to them to satisfy their needs accurately.

CHAPTER FIVE

Quantitative and qualitative approaches marketing gathering method

Critically evaluate the relative merits of quantitative and qualitative approaches to data collection for a large retailer.

The marketing research process needs to follow these steps: defining the problem and research objectives, developing the research plan, collecting the data, analyzing the data, then presenting the findings.

In general, the specific marketing research major activities include: Research into customer needs and expectation and a variety of qualitative techniques are used to study the often complex sets of expectations that customers have with respect to a purchase. For example, when buying a personal computer, what are customers' expectation with respect to reliability, after -sales support, design etc? Customer satisfaction surveys indicate customer areas of satisfaction or dissatisfaction; how spending money on various forms of communication, such as advertising, sales promotion, and public relations; researching similar industry studies about competitors in completely unrelated business sectors how to improve own marketing effectiveness; researching key client studies about number of customers how to make special efforts to ensure that these customers are satisfied with its standards of service and prices; researching into intermediaries, such as agents dealers are close to consumers to gather information about consumers' needs and expectation. For example in relation to reliability, delivery times and after sales services; researching front line employees their attitude towards the company and researching environmental scanning changing on trends to influence the company development in the future. Structure of market research includes spending on market research, types of market research and potential problem. Market research means researching the the immediate competitive environment of the marketplace, including customers, competitors, suppliers, distributors and retailer. Otherwise, marketing research includes all the above and companies and their strategies and markets of whose products sale or services provision and the wider environment within which operates (e.g. political, social, economic etc factor influences). Hence, marketing research means the systematic design, collection, analysis and reporting of data and finding relevant to a specific marketing situation facing the organization. In general, the ten most common market research activities for a large retailer data collection, include determination of market characteristics, measurement of market potential, market share analysis, sales analysis, studies of business trends, short range forecasting, competitive product studies, long range forecasting, pricing studies and testing existing products.

The reasons why a large retailer needs to conduct that research in new product development include the product must appeal to the customer, timely market research can help the large retailer to predict its client's needs/wants, market research tends to point out success and failure before its product is launched for real and it can save its money and time. A large retailer's market research can be sources by either primary or secondary or both and it can use either qualitative or quantitative or both methodologies and it can achieve objectives either exploratory or descriptive or causal experimental.

The primary source is collection of data specifically for the problem or project in hand and the secondary source is based on data previously collected for purposes other than the research in hand. e.g. published articles, governments etc.

On the quantitative benefits hand, it is cheaper to sample size ; probabilities in depth motivations and feelings, it allows managers to observe real client reaction to the issue, e.g. comments and associations regard a new product fresh from the laboratory. It often used precursor to quantitative research, it can give the research department a low cost and timely sense of which issues in quantitative research. Quantitative research is designed to gather information from statistically representative samples of target population. The sample size is related to the size of the total population being studied, the variability within it, and the degree of statistically reliability required, balanced against time and cost constraints. It includes these skilful analyses such as below:

Correlation analysis means two phenomena are associated with each other. For example, whether change in household income is associated with the amount that a household spends on eating out of or firm's advertising expenditure on a product and sale revenue for it's relationship. Regression analysis means to use to build a model of causes (independent variables), which lead to an effect (the dependent variable). Companies shall use a historical database to test models that are assessed for the amount of variance in the dataset that they explain. Analysis of variance is used to test hypotheses about differences between two or more means. It is widely used in experimental frameworks where the researcher wished to examine the effects of two or more treatments on customers.

Conjoint analysis can provide valuable information for market segmentation, new product development, forecasting and pricing decisions and it can analyze the real life trade off that shoppers make when evaluating a range of features that are present in a range of product. Cluster analysis is frequently used in segmentation studies, but does not provide the marketer with a unique solutions.

Neural network analysis splits a dataset into a training set and a testing set. However, quantitative analysis techniques can suffer from a number of weakness , such as sampling error, measurement error, significant estimation of sample population error, inappropriate estimation of population may be validated statistical tests and inappropriate interpretation of results can highly subjective.

On the qualitative merits hand, large retailer can get merits, such as many sample size and questions and information per respondent and much application of questioner's skill, analyst's skill and type of analysis. Qualitative techniques essentially seek to recreate the listening ear and interpretative mind that so many entrepreneurs use so well. Qualitative marketing research involves the exploration and interpretation of the perceptions and behavior of small samples of individuals and the study of the motivators behind observed actions. It can be highly focused, exploring in depth, for example, the attitudes that buyers have towards particular brand names. The techniques used to encourage respondents to speak and behave honestly. However, it is difficult to assess the validity of qualitative research techniques, and the tests for significance that are available for most quantitative techniques are largely lacking for qualitative techniques.

The quantitative and qualitative approaches to data collection for a large retailer its merits can achieve objective is either by exploratory, it means preliminary data needed to develop an idea further, e.g. outline concepts, gather insights, formulate hypotheses; it is either by descriptive, it means to describe an element of an ideas precisely, e.g. who is the target market, how large is it, how will it develops ; it is either by causal, it means to test a cause and effect relationship, e.g. price elasticity is by experiment. Moreover, the quantitative and qualitative approaches to data collection can help a large retailer to find methods how to solve problems to raise competition confidently. In the beginning, of the market research process step, it needs to define the problem and objectives, such as it needs to distinguish between it's research type needed, e.g. exploratory descriptive or causal . Then, it needs to develop the research plan, such as deciding on budget, data sources, research approaches and instruments, sampling plan and contact methods. Next, it needs to collect information, such as information is collected according to the plan. Following step, it needs to analyze the information , such as statistical manipulation of the data collected, e.g. regression or subjective analysis of focus group. Final step, it needs to present the findings, such as overall conclusion to be presented rather than statistical methodologies.

Data collection gathers for a large retailer, it can gather syndicated data from householders, it is gathered either by psychographics and lifestyle, advertising, evaluation etc. styles of surveys and use panels or both sources. Primary data is originated by a researcher for the specific purpose of addressing the problem at hand, the collection of primary data involves all six steps of the marketing research process as well as secondary data has already been collected for purposes other than the problem at hand. These data can be located quickly and inexpensively. The intention to uses of secondary data for a large retailer, it aims to identify the problem and better defines the problem, develops an approach to the problem, formulates an appropriates research design, for example by identifying the key variables, answers certain research questions and test some hypotheses and interprets primary data more insightfully.

On qualitative merits to secondary data collection for a large retailer. The criteria aspect, this data collection method can give merits of response rate, quality and analysis data, sampling technique and size, questionnaire design, fieldwork benefits to a large retailer, so it's data should be reliable, valid to the problem; on error and errors in approach, research design, sampling , data collection and analysis and reporting, so it can assess accuracy by comparing data from different sources. On currency aspect, this data collection method can assess time lag between collection and publication, frequency of updates, so census data are updated by syndicated large retailer; on objective aspect, secondary data collection method can help large retailer to judge whether the data collected were needed to used for which parts of market strategies benefits for consumer research, so the objective determines the relevance of data; on nature aspect, this data collection method can define key variables, units of measurement, categories used, relationships examined, so it can reconfigure the data to increase a large retailer market strategies benefits usefulness and on dependability aspect, this data collection method provides expertise, credibility, reputation and trustworthiness of the source, so it's data should be obtained from an original source to raise market research benefits to a large retailer. Hence, internal secondary data collection can help large retailer department project to store project to analyze sales by product line, by major department, e.g. men's wear, by specific stores by geographical region, by cash versus credit purchased, sales in specific time periods, by size of purchase and trends in many of these classifications were also examined.

Secondary data collection can include demographic data, which is type of individual household level data available from consumers, such as identification, e.g. name, address, telephone , sex, marital status, age, income, occupation etc. as well as psychographic lifestyle data, such as consumer personal interest. Hence, a large retailer can get this quantitative and qualitative data to judge whether who is segmentation target to compete in its business market. For example, market research demands cooperation and trust between the client commissioning a study and the company carrying it out.

The reputation that a market research agency has built for itself
is particularly important where qualitative research is involved as well as qualitative research techniques are utilizing quasi quantitative technique in order to enhance their credibility.

In conclusion, large retailers are reliance on customer's view due to many experienced larger retailers are relying more on interactive development with lead clients. Because traditional market research for truly innovative new products have frequently proved misleading. Hence, quantitative and qualitative approaches must need to use to gather to assess how to achieve marketing strategies timely and objectively and relevant to win whose competitors nowadays.

2. Discuss the limitation of statistically based consumer databases of the type discussed here. Do qualitative approaches based on small groups offer any advantages?

Any large retailers need to follow this process to use marketing information system to gather data from consumer databases. First step, which need to gather data either from internal data or external data source or both. The internal data includes enquires, orders, customer complaints etc. as well as the external data is from customer panels, intermediaries etc. Next step, the marketing information system will carry on processes as data collection and analyzing internal data. Final step, the marketing information system will produce outcomes, such as input to decision support system and data for decision makers to evaluate and storage of data in a data warehouse outcomes. A large retailer can collect consumer data computerized database, from online bibliographic database or from internet numeric databases, full text database or offline directory databases, special purpose databases. Hence, computerized published external secondary sources can help large retailers to identify individuals or organizations to collect specific data, for example, consultants and consulting organization directory, directory of market research reports, studies and surveys and research services directory and gather indices to help in locating information on a particular topic in several different publications. Hence, large retailer can collect classification of computerized databases include bibliographic databases are composed of citations to articles, numeric databases contain numerical and statistical information , full -text databases contain the complete text of the source documents comprising the database, directory databases provide information on individuals or organizations and services and special purpose database provide specialized information. Hence, large retailer can get syndicated service to collect and sell common pools of data of known commercial value designed to serve a number of clients and syndicated sources can be classified based on the unit of measurement (households/consumers) and institutions two groups. Syndicated services of householders/ consumers include surveys, data collection is from psychographic and lifestyles, general and advertising evaluation as well as it also include panels data collection is from purchase and media of volume tracking data and scanner diary panels as well as it also include electronic scanner services is from scanner diary panels with cable television.

Potential problems to limitation with market research of statistically based customer data bases include, small groups do not know when and how to do research from database and problems exist with research buyers and suppliers and it needs frequent techniques and small groups exist problems with traditional market research effort. On limitation of when and how not to conduct market research issue, it includes lack of resources, closed mindset, poor timing arrangement in marketplace, research results are not actionable, late timing is process, unclear objectives and cost outweighs benefits limitation. On the lack of resources occasion issue, if quantitative research is needed, it is not worth doing unless a statistically significant sample can be used, On the research results, small groups' clients are difficult to get psychographic data from statistically based consumer databases to analyze to carry on market research. On the closed mindset limitation issue, when research is used as a preconceived idea. The statistically based consumer databases needs long time to gather data to analyze to carry on marketing research in its process. It cause poor timing to give clients to find marketing research result, if the client wants to know whether who ought to invest to develop the new product to promote to the marketing to sell from statistically based consumer database in the short time.

On cost outweighs benefits limitation, the statistically based consumer databases expected value of the information gathering time and resources spending cost should outweigh the cost of gathering the data from normal marketing research method.

On the limitation of problems with research statistically based customer databases , qualitative limitations include narrow concept of research, unrealistic view of timeframe, as well as variable quality of market researchers and it is possible that market researchers have not own sufficient technical to apply statistically based customer data bases. For example, market researchers will feel difficult to find facts from statistically customer data bases and who will spend much time to define research result from finding.

The qualitative approaches based on small groups offer any advantages from statistically marketing research customer databases only, but small groups can not offer any advantages from statistically market research customer databases. The reason is due to market research is about determining the characteristics of a market, for example, in terms of its size, requirements, growth rate, market segments and competitor positioning. Otherwise, marketing research is broader and is about researching the whole of a company's marketing activities. In most organizations, such search would probably include monitoring the effectiveness of its advertising, intermediates, and pricing position. Hence, small groups need to focus on marketing researching its company's internal marketing activities, such as pricing strategy, advertising method. Due to small groups are not large organizations, which did not focus on market research to external marketing environment, such as growth rate, market segment etc influences. However, statistically based customer databases also have these qualitative approaches to small groups offer advantages include, easy of completion, realism, comprehensive, per-testing, questioner training, respondent motivation, repetition, cultural issues, bias in formulation and sensitivity of question etc. qualitative approaches.

3. What effects do you expect the development of interactive electronic media to have on retailers' collection of marketing research information from consumers?

The effects that I expect the development of interactive electronic media to have on retailer's collection of marketing research information from consumers. Limited use of market research indicated formal market analyses continue to be

useful for extending product lines, but they are often misleading when applied to radical innovations. Problems, with traditional market research has allowed prominent product failures and wrong predictions; markets are increasingly becoming micro-segmented, e.g. sports shoes aimed at fashion conscious women specifically for aerobic, so mass market research becomes correspondingly irrelevant; it is helpful for improvements, but traditional market research method is less for radical innovations and is less for more accurate targeting. Thus, I expect the development of interactive electronic media effects to have on retailers collection of marketing research in formation from consumers. It may be advantageous to analyze continue to be useful for expanding product lines in the most short time and it will not mislead to businessmen when who applied this electronic media on retailers collection of marketing research method to get radical innovations accurately. For example, predicting whether who are major targeting segments for the sport shoe company to sell in the short time accurately, such as between 10 ages and 30 ages young male client group or young female client group or between 31 ages to 50 ages adult male client group or adult female client group.

On the evaluating internet resources for retailer's collection of marketing research legal hand, it needs to indicate the content of a resource must be reflective. If there is change, the resource must promptly reflect that change; if a law has been amended, any discussion on the web must reflect the law as amended. Otherwise, the internet resource is not qualified for citation in legal marketing research; research specialization and achievement, institutional and professional affiliation, medium of communication, e.g. professional journal and publishers are all useful criteria to evaluate credibility; questions to ask include: Is it a reviewed articles? Is it a law review journal? And does the author exhibit critical assessment of a resource? ; Copyrighted work means that an individual or an institution could claim ownership, responsibility and liability for the resource. It also publication and therefore users may have to comply with the principle of fair value; resources with citations journalistic ones. Researchers should therefore accord higher preference to resources with citations; many web resources disappear with the resources who contain. For instance, an electronically published law report must not only be current but also be continuous for it to be a dependable source for consultation, it is important to examine whether a resource reflects the attributed of misinformation half truths prejudice; a marketing researcher needs resources that can be connected to individual retailer or company's resources. In general, online market researchers know that search engineers vary in how who select ranking of results. With the advent of search engine optimization and the role of online marketing search engines, results are impacted by things other than returning results that are customized to rank higher sponsored links, with the page owner paying advertising dollars to get their site ranked higher. General search engines can be helpful when getting started or determining the scope of a particular question. Search engines like Google, Yahoo can be powerful tools. It is good practice to not rely on only one general search engine. General research engines, like Google, also have power helpful in narrowing large search results.

An old librarian advertisement page is that customers can have something quick, cheap and accurate but who can only pick two out three. Therefore, choosing the top two most important factors will help consumers decide between conducting an open web marketing search and using specialized commercial databases. However, law firm librarians need to play important roles in helping their firms and staff members locate, manage and use internet resources efficiently and cost effectively and who need to understand not only the needs of their firms and clients, but also the specific types of information available online as well as offline to meet clients' unique needs and who also need to help business firms grow and strength their client services by taking advantage of the rich information online. For instance, law librarians need to lead the form in creating the best and most comprehensive combination of knowledge and information re-sources, including capturing and preserving reliable free and low cost internet resources, that accommodates the firm's budget and user needs, maintain the firm's intranet, further enabling cost effective online legal research, promote free and low cost online resources and research techniques, whenever, feasible to help attorneys and staffs improve research efficiency and cost effectiveness, manage electronic subscriptions which now generally account for a large annual spending than books and newsletters, educate users and conduct training sessions on online research skills, provide tailored content for individual users or groups to facilitate intelligent filtering of the abundance of available information online, provide guideline on the usefulness and reliability of legal resources, guide attorneys as well as consumers in finding information from the internet efficiently.

On evaluating internet research surveys marketing research hand, there have advantages of internet research surveys, rather than mailing a paper survey, a respondent can be given a hyperlink to a web site containing the survey or in an email survey, a questionnaire is sent to a respondent via electronic mail, possibly as an attachment . Electronic media survey is as an alternative to conventional survey modes , e.g. the telephone, mail and face to face interviewing. For example, a web survey can relatively simply incorporate multi-media graphics and sound into the survey instrument, automatic branching and real time randomization of survey questions and/ or answers into self administered web surveys. However, unlike when phone and mail surveys were first introduced, concerned exist about whether these internet based surveys are scientifically valid and how they are the best conducted. Because internet can offer possibility of multimedia and interactive surveys containing audio and video, convenience samples to respondents email address. As a result, quick polls and other types of entertainment surveys have become increasingly popular and widespread on the web marketing research.

On the web marketing based surveys had particular three of benefit assumptions to attract companies to choose to do marketing research: (a) internet based surveys are much cheaper to conduct, (b) internet based surveys are faster, (c) when combined with other survey modes, internet based surveys yield higher response rates than conventional survey modes by themselves. In general, companies shall consider the following key characteristics of surveys choices: Response rate, timeliness, data quality and cost .

(Adrian, P. 2012) indicated that in response rate hand, web surveys respondents that can or will answer via the web may not be sufficiently large to compare mail surveys possibly. However, a company AT& T employees surveys experiment indicated to report a 63% response rate via email (63 returned not of 100 sent by email) compared to a 38% response rate for postal mail (14 returned out of 40 sent by mail). Interestingly, it indicated the response rates to the fast that, at the time, At& T employees received a lot of corporate paper junk mail yet over the internal email system, they received little to no electronic junk mail. I expect the development of interactive electronic media market research survey can achieve responses from a convenience sample might be useful in developing research hypotheses. Responses from convenience samples might also be useful for identifying issues, defining ranges of alternatives or collecting other sorts of non inferential data.

On timeliness hand, survey timeliness is increasingly stressed. The length of time it takes to field a survey is a function of the contact, response and follow up modes. the relevant measure is not average response time, but maximum response time (or perhaps some large percentage of the response time distribution) since survey analysis generally does not begin until all of the responses are in. However, simply concluding that internet based surveys are faster than mail surveys ignores the reality that the total amount of time for survey fielding time is more than just the survey response time. A complete comparison must take into account the mode of contact and how long that process will take and the made of follow up allowing for multiple follow up contact periods. For example, if email address of respondents are unavailable and a probability sample is desired than respondents may have to be contacted by mail. In this case a web survey only saves time for the return delivery of the completed questionnaire and not for the contact and follow up, so that the resulting time savings may only be a fraction of the total survey fielding time. For example, a internet survey company, knowledge networks has indicated that to achieve 70 to 80 % response rates they must leave a survey in the field for about 10 days. This period comprises one workweek with two weekends because they find that most respondents complete their surveys on the weekend (Adrian, P. 2012).

In conclusion, the delivery time of an internet based survey is faster than the delivery of a survey by mail, it does not necessarily follow that the increased delivery speed will translate into a significantly shorter survey fielding period. Two points are relevant: dramatic possible for specialized populations and even for populations in which all electronic surveys are possible.

On the quality hand, the primary purpose of a survey is to gather information about a population , the information is useless unless it is accurate and representative of the population. When survey error is commonly characterized in terms of the precision of statistical estimated, a good survey designing seeks to reduce all types of errors, including coverage, sampling, non response and measurement errors. Data quality includes unit and item non response, honesty of responses , particularly for questions of a sensitive nature, completeness of responses particularly for open ended questions and quality of data transcription into an electronic format for analysis of requires by the survey made. Data quality is usually measured by the number of respondents with missing items or the questions, longer answered are usually considered more informative and of higher quality email surveys may incur a higher percentage of items missing than mail surveys. Other quality issues for internet based surveys resulting from some sort of sampling errors are generally the same as for conventional surveys. However, such accuracy may be misleading if non response biases are not accounted for and researchers need to carefully consider the trade offs between smaller samples that allow for careful non response follow up and larger samples with less or no follow up. Web surveys can be programmed to conduct input validation as a logical check of the respondent's answers.These types of checks improve data quality and subsequently save time in the preparation of the analysis file. This will eliminate errors and from the respondent's point of view, simplify the process of taking the survey.

On cost hand, designing a survey fundamentally involves making trade off between the quality and quantity of data and cost. For smaller research surveys that are not subsidized in any way, a major component of total survey cost is frequently the researcher's time for survey design and subsequent data analysis. The labour cost of the personnel who actually execute the survey. It depends on the size of the survey and the complexity of the design either researcher labour cost, survey personnel labour costs or a combination of the two will likely dominate the survey budget.When lower costs are often of the benefits, of internet based surveys, Couper et al. (1999) found no cost benefit in email compared to postal mail surveys in their work. In a large and comprehensive survey effort of different government agencies. Couper et al. compared an all email survey (contract, response and follow up) versus an all mail survey. They found that evaluating and testing the email software took over 150 hours almost 4 times as much as they budgeted.

For the mail survey, costs for printing and posting were \$1.6 per reply and data editing and entry cost about \$1.81 . For the mail survey , managing the email cost \$1.74 per completed case. In addition, they handled over 900 toll free call of a technical nature when the printing and mailing costs were eliminated for the email survey. Couper et al.(1999) found that the cost of evaluating and testing the email software, additional post collection processing and the cost of maintaining a toll free phone line which was largely dedicated to responding to technical questions related to the email surveys offset any savings. For example, email survey was designed so that respondents would use the reply function of their email program so the resulting replies could be automatically read into a database upon receipt.

I expect web marketing based surveys can reduce errors to avoid to mislead companies to find the wrong marketing strategy to compare paper surveys from every time of individual group customer questionnaires researches from internet. Moreover, I also expect web marketing based surveys can reduce cost to compare paper surveys from every time of group customer questionnaires researches from internet. In conclusion, I expect the development of interactive electronic media to have on retailers collection of marketing research information from consumers, the internet companies need to consider the electronic surveys response rate and time and quality and cost and legal responsibilities issues to let any companies to use their electronic media to carry on marketing research from customers to feel more satisfactory to compare to traditional questionnaires market research media if internet companies still hoped business companies still chose to use whose service to do marketing research in the future.

References

Ambady, N. and Rosenthal, R.(1992)' Thin Silces Of Behavior As Predictors Of Interpersonal Consequences: A meta-analysis, psychological Bulletin, 2: 256-74

Arnade, E. (2014) Journal Of Consumer Research, Make a face: Implict and explict measurement of facial expression by orange juices using face reading technology. Food quality and preference, vol.32, p.161-172. Retrieved: http://hdl.handle.net/10919/54538.

Carrere, S. and Gottman, J. (1999) ' predicting divorce amongnewlyweds from the first three minutes of a marital conflice discussion', family processes 38:293-301.

Hung & Mukhopadhyay.(June 2012), Emotion And Consumer Behavior, , vol. 40 no.5 (June 2012), 39-50.

Meservy, T.O. jnsen, M.L. Kruse, W.J., Burgoo, J.K. and Nunamaker Jr., J.F. (2008) ' Automatic extraction of deceptive behavioral cues from video', in H.Chen, E. Reid, J. Sinai, A. Silke and B. Ganor (eds) Terrorism Informatics (pp. 495-516), New York: Springer.

Miller, K. (2012), Consumer behavior, Washington, USA. Retrieved: http://www.amazon.com

Palmer (2012), Consumer behavior and credit card payment, Journal of management market resarch.

Webb et. al (2000), The impact of perceived corporate social responsibility on consumer behavior, Journal of business research 59(1): pp. 46-53 Jan. 2006.